ENGLISCH LERNEN DURCH
Tiergeschichten

Simo Edu

Hallo, junge Entdeckerin / junger Entdecker!

Mach dich bereit für eine lustige Reise in die Welt der Tiere. Dieses Buch von Simo Edu wurde entwickelt, um dir zu helfen, Englisch auf spielerische und spannende Weise zu lernen. Du wirst lustige Geschichten lesen, Spiele spielen und kreativ werden!

So ist jede Tier-Geschichte aufgebaut:
Jedes Kapitel folgt fünf einfachen und unterhaltsamen Schritten:

1. Lies die Geschichte
Jeder Teil des Buches beginnt mit einer einfachen und lustigen Geschichte auf Englisch über ein besonderes Tier.

2. Lerne neue Wörter
Nach der Geschichte findest du 10 wichtige Vokabeln aus dem Text. Wir haben sie für dich ins Deutsche übersetzt, damit du sie perfekt verstehst.

3. Spiele das Wortsuchspiel
Finde die neuen englischen Wörter in einem lustigen Wortsuchrätsel! Das ist eine tolle Methode, um sie dir zu merken.

4. Beantworte die Fragen

Als Nächstes kannst du dein Gedächtnis mit ein paar einfachen Verständnisfragen zur Geschichte testen, die du gerade gelesen hast.

5. Zeit zum Ausmalen!

Zum Schluss kannst du dich entspannen und das Tier mit einer schönen Malvorlage zum Leben erwecken. Benutze deine Lieblingsfarben!

Und das ist noch nicht alles!

Nachdem du alle Tiere kennengelernt hast, gibt es am Ende des Buches weitere Aktivitäten. Hier übst du noch mehr Vokabeln zum Thema Tiere und lernst einige wichtige englische Grammatikregeln, die dich zu einem Super-Sprecher machen!

Dieses Buch ist perfekt für Lernende auf dem A1/A2-Niveau.

Viel Spaß beim Lernen und Malen.

Max the Brave Mouse

Max is a small mouse.
He lives in a hole in the wall.
One day, he hears a loud noise.
It is a big, scary cat!
Max hides behind a chair.
The cat looks around.
Max stays very still.
The cat leaves the room.
Max runs back to his hole.
He is safe and happy.

English Word	German
small	klein
hole	Loch
wall	Wand
noise	Geräusch
scary	unheimlich / gruselig
hides	versteckt sich
chair	Stuhl
leaves (the room)	verlässt (den Raum)
runs	rennt
safe	sicher

T	H	G	P	C	H	A	I	R	Q
A	Z	V	O	L	M	X	Y	B	T
C	W	U	H	O	L	E	E	A	E
A	K	L	I	N	D	P	P	P	M
T	B	C	A	T	F	U	E	O	T
L	P	E	D	U	C	Q	M	R	Y
R	A	S	O	M	U	O	L	U	T
J	H	M	O	U	S	E	G	Y	I
K	R	E	J	K	L	N	X	F	A
W	Q	P	H	A	P	P	Y	S	Z

mouse, hole, cat, chair, happy

What animal is Max?

Where does Max live?

Why does Max hide?

What does Max do when
the cat leaves?

Was Max brave?

Lily the Singing Bird

Lily is a little yellow bird.
She loves to sing in the morning.
She lives in a tall tree.
All the animals stop to listen.
Her song is sweet and soft.
The sun shines on her feathers.
A squirrel claps for her.
The rabbits dance below.
Lily sings every day.
Everyone loves
her music.

English Word	German
bird	Vogel
yellow	gelb
sing	singen
tree	Baum
animals	Tiere
song	Lied
feathers	Federn
squirrel	Eichhörnchen
rabbits	Kaninchen
music	Musik

Y	T	R	E	E	N	S	M	P	D
X	E	Q	L	I	L	Y	E	A	O
B	F	E	A	T	H	E	R	S	L
T	K	S	Z	W	Y	G	D	I	T
U	S	I	N	G	V	B	U	O	R
P	R	F	T	J	O	E	L	L	A
Q	Y	E	L	L	O	W	N	U	N
V	D	C	H	X	M	J	K	L	B
H	A	I	M	Z	Q	I	P	O	G
E	W	R	E	T	S	A	F	S	C

lily, yellow, tree, feathers, sing

What color is Lily?

What does she love to do?

Where does she live?

Who claps for her?

Do the animals like her song?

Toby the Sleepy Turtle

Toby is a turtle.
He moves very slowly.
He loves to sleep under the sun.
One day, it starts to rain.
Toby wakes up and runs!
But turtles can't run fast.
He finds a big leaf.
He hides under it.
The rain stops soon.
Toby goes back to sleep.

English Word	**German**
turtle	Schildkröte
moves	bewegt sich
slowly	langsam
sleep	schlafen
sun	Sonne
rain	Regen
wakes	wacht auf
runs	rennt
leaf	Blatt
hides	versteckt sich

T	U	R	T	L	E	P	Q	W	E
S	L	O	W	L	Y	R	A	I	N
L	M	N	O	P	Q	R	S	L	A
E	E	A	F	L	E	A	F	B	C
E	A	S	L	E	E	P	X	Y	Z
P	O	I	U	Y	T	R	E	W	Q
A	S	D	F	G	H	J	K	L	M
N	B	V	C	X	Z	Q	W	E	R
Q	W	E	R	T	Y	U	I	O	P
A	S	D	F	G	H	J	K	L	M

turtle, slowly, sleep, rain, leaf

What kind of animal is Toby?

What does he love to do?

Why does he wake up?

What does Toby hide under?

What happens after the rain?

Sam the Happy Dog

Sam is a brown dog.
He has a big smile.
He plays with a red ball.
He runs in the grass.
He jumps in the mud.
He shakes off the water.
A boy laughs and hugs him.
They play all day.
Sam is tired and happy.
He dreams of balls and bones.

English Word	German
dog	Hund
smile	Lächeln
ball	Ball
grass	Gras
mud	Schlamm
shakes	schüttelt sich
water	Wasser
laughs	lacht
hugs	umarmt
bones	Knochen

T	U	R	T	L	E	P	Q	W	E
S	L	O	W	L	Y	R	A	I	N
L	M	N	O	P	Q	R	S	L	A
E	E	A	F	L	E	A	F	B	C
E	A	S	L	E	E	P	X	Y	Z
P	O	I	U	Y	T	R	E	W	Q
A	S	D	F	G	H	J	K	L	M
N	B	V	C	X	Z	Q	W	E	R
Q	W	E	R	T	Y	U	I	O	P
A	S	D	F	G	H	J	K	L	M

dog, smile, ball, mud, bones

What color is Sam?

What does Sam play with?

Where does he run?

Who hugs Sam?

What does Sam dream about?

Bella the Shy Bunny

Bella is a white bunny.
She is very shy.
She hides behind flowers.
A butterfly flies near.
Bella watches it dance.
The butterfly lands on her nose.
Bella giggles.
She jumps with joy.
Now she wants to play.
She is not shy anymore.

English Word	German
bunny	Häschen
shy	schüchtern
hides	versteckt sich
flowers	Blumen
butterfly	Schmetterling
flies	fliegt
lands	landet
nose	Nase
giggles	kichert
joy	Freude

B	U	N	N	Y	T	R	E	W	Q
F	L	O	W	E	R	S	M	L	K
P	A	S	D	F	G	H	J	S	N
L	K	J	O	Y	U	I	O	Z	O
O	I	U	Y	T	R	E	W	S	S
W	Q	N	O	S	E	A	B	D	E
E	F	G	H	J	K	L	Z	X	C
R	T	Y	U	I	O	P	M	N	V
S	H	Y	A	B	C	D	E	F	B
M	N	B	V	C	X	Z	Q	W	A

bunny, shy, nose, joy, flowers

What kind of animal is Bella?

Where does she hide?

What lands on her nose?

How does Bella feel at the end?

Is she still shy?

Leo the Lion Learns to Share

Leo is a strong lion.
He has a red ball.
He does not want to share.
A zebra asks to play.
Leo says "No!"
The zebra walks away.
Leo feels sad.
He calls the zebra back.
They play together.
Leo is happy now.

English Word	German
lion	Löwe
strong	stark
share	teilen
zebra	Zebra
asks	fragt
says	sagt
walks	geht
feels	fühlt
calls	ruft
together	zusammen

L	I	O	N	G	H	J	K	L
Z	E	B	R	A	S	A	D	F
P	Q	W	E	R	T	Y	U	I
S	T	R	O	N	G	M	N	B
S	H	A	R	E	V	C	X	Z
G	F	D	S	A	Q	W	E	R
T	Y	U	I	O	P	L	K	J
M	N	B	V	C	X	Z	A	S
Q	W	E	R	T	Y	U	I	O
A	S	D	F	G	H	J	K	L

lion, zebra, share, sad, strong

What does Leo have?

Who wants to play with Leo?

What does Leo say first?

Why does Leo feel sad?

What do they do at the end?

Nina the Nice Cow

Nina is a big cow.
She loves helping others.
A duck can't reach a branch.
Nina bends the tree down.
The duck gets an apple.
"Thank you, Nina!" says the duck.
A cat drops her toy.
Nina gives it back.
Everyone smiles at Nina.
She is kind and happy.

English Word	German
cow	Kuh
helping	helfen
duck	Ente
branch	Ast
bends	biegt
apple	Apfel
cat	Katze
toy	Spielzeug
kind	freundlich
smiles	lächeln

C	O	W	Q	W	E	R	T	Y
A	P	P	L	E	M	N	B	V
D	U	C	K	A	S	D	F	G
L	K	J	H	G	F	D	S	A
T	O	Y	X	Z	C	V	B	N
Q	W	E	R	T	Y	U	I	O
M	N	B	V	C	X	Z	L	P
A	S	D	F	G	H	J	K	L
K	I	N	D	Q	W	E	R	T
U	I	O	P	L	K	J	H	G

cow, duck, apple, toy, kind

What animal is Nina?

Who needs help first?

What does Nina do?

Who drops a toy?

Is Nina helpful?

the Brave Dinosaur

Danny is a green dinosaur.
He wakes up in the forest.
He eats leaves from tall trees.
Danny walks by a river.
He sees a group of small dinosaurs.
They are scared.
A loud roar comes from a cave!
Danny stands tall and looks.
It is just a big wind.
Everyone laughs.
Danny is happy and keeps walking.

English Word	German
dinosaur	Dinosaurier
forest	Wald
leaves	Blätter
river	Fluss
group	Gruppe
scared	verängstigt
roar	Gebrüll
cave	Höhle
wind	Wind
laugh	lachen

D	I	N	O	Q	W	E	R	T
L	E	A	V	E	S	S	D	F
B	N	M	C	A	V	E	G	H
P	O	I	U	Y	T	R	O	A
R	O	A	R	L	K	J	H	G
W	I	N	D	A	S	D	F	G
Z	X	C	V	B	N	M	Q	W
U	I	O	P	L	K	J	H	G
T	R	E	E	S	M	N	B	V
Q	W	E	R	T	Y	U	I	O

dino, leaves, roar, cave, wind

What kind of animal is Danny?

Where does Danny wake up?

What does Danny eat?

Where does Danny walk?

How does Danny feel at the end?

The Strong Ant

Andy is a little ant.
He lives in the ground.
Andy is very strong.
He carries food every day.
He walks in a line with his friends.
They work together.
Andy finds a big crumb.
He pulls it home.
The queen ant is happy.
Andy smiles. He loves to help.

English Word	German
ant	Ameise
ground	Boden
strong	stark
carries	trägt
line	Reihe / Linie
friends	Freunde
crumb	Krümel
pulls	zieht
queen	Königin
help	helfen

A	N	T	Q	W	E	R	T	Y
C	R	U	M	B	S	D	F	G
L	K	J	H	G	F	D	Q	Z
Q	U	E	E	N	M	N	B	V
P	U	L	L	S	X	C	V	B
S	T	R	O	N	G	A	S	D
F	R	I	E	N	D	S	L	K
U	I	O	P	L	K	J	H	G
M	N	B	V	C	X	Z	A	S
Q	W	E	R	T	Y	U	I	O

ant, crumb, queen, pulls, strong

What kind of animal is Andy?

What makes Andy special?

Where does Andy live?

What does Andy carry?

What does Andy find?

Freddy the Fish's Big Jump

Freddy is a fast fish.
He lives in a pond.
He sees a fly above the water.
He wants to eat it.
He jumps very high.
Splash! He misses.
He tries again.
This time, he gets the fly.
Freddy is proud.
He swims in circles.

English Word	German
fish	Fisch
fast	schnell
pond	Teich
fly (insect)	Fliege
water	Wasser
jumps	springt
misses	verfehlt
proud	stolz
swims	schwimmt
circles	Kreise

F	I	S	H	T	Y	U	I	O
P	O	N	D	A	S	D	F	G
L	K	J	H	G	F	L	Y	Q
M	N	B	V	C	X	Z	A	W
J	U	M	P	S	M	N	B	V
Q	W	E	R	T	Y	U	I	O
P	R	O	U	D	K	J	H	G
A	S	D	F	G	H	J	K	L
Z	X	C	V	B	N	M	Q	W
E	R	T	Y	U	I	O	P	L

fish, pond, fly, jumps, proud

What kind of animal is Freddy?

Where does he live?

What does he try to catch?

Does he get the fly the first time?

How does Freddy feel?

Cindy the Clever Cat

Cindy is a smart cat.
She loves to explore.
One day, she finds a box.
What's inside?
It's a ball of yarn!
She bats it with her paw.
The yarn rolls fast.
She chases it around.
She makes a mess!
But she has fun.

English Word	German
smart	klug
explore	erkunden
box	Schachtel
inside	drinnen
yarn	Garn
bats (hits)	schlägt (mit der Pfote)
paw	Pfote
rolls	rollt
chases	jagt
mess	Unordnung

S	M	A	R	T	X	Y	Z	A
B	O	X	P	L	M	N	O	B
Y	A	R	N	Q	W	E	R	C
D	F	G	H	J	K	L	H	H
P	A	W	A	S	D	F	G	A
T	Y	U	I	O	P	A	S	S
L	K	J	H	G	F	D	C	E
M	N	B	V	C	X	Z	H	S
A	S	D	F	G	H	J	K	E
Q	W	E	R	T	Y	U	I	S

smart, box, yarn, paw, chases

What animal is Cindy?

What does she find?

What does she do with the yarn?

Is it a clean or messy game?

Does she have fun?

Oscar the Owl at Night

Oscar is an owl.
He wakes up at night.
He sees stars in the sky.
He flies above the trees.
He hears a frog croak.
He sees a mouse below.
But Oscar is not hungry.
He just wants to look.
He loves the quiet night.
Oscar is wise and calm.

English Word	German
owl	Eule
night	Nacht
stars	Sterne
sky	Himmel
flies	fliegt
trees	Bäume
hears	hört
croak	quaken
quiet	ruhig
calm	gelassen

O	W	L	Q	W	E	R	T	Y
S	T	A	R	S	A	S	D	F
L	K	J	H	G	F	L	I	E
F	L	I	E	S	B	N	M	G
N	I	G	H	T	V	C	X	Z
Q	W	E	R	T	Y	U	I	O
A	S	D	F	G	H	J	K	L
Z	X	C	V	B	N	M	Q	W
C	A	L	M	L	K	J	H	G
U	I	O	P	A	S	D	F	G

owl, stars, flies, night, calm

What animal is Oscar?

When does he wake up?

What does he hear?

Is Oscar hungry?

How does Oscar feel?

Daisy the Dancing Duck

Daisy is a white duck.
She loves to dance in the rain.
She splashes in puddles.
Her wings flap with joy.
Frogs jump with her.
The sky is gray, but Daisy smiles.
She spins and quacks.
The wind sings with her.
Everyone watches her dance.
She bows at the end.

English Word	German
duck	Ente
dance	tanzen
rain	Regen
puddles	Pfützen
wings	Flügel
flap	flattern
frogs	Frösche
spins	dreht sich
quacks	quakt
bows	verbeugt sich

D	A	N	C	E	Q	W	E	R
B	O	W	S	A	S	D	F	G
L	K	J	H	G	F	D	A	Q
Q	U	A	C	K	S	M	N	B
P	O	I	U	Y	T	R	A	I
N	M	B	V	C	X	Z	N	N
W	I	N	G	S	L	K	J	H
E	R	T	Y	U	I	O	P	Z
A	S	D	F	G	H	J	K	X
Q	W	E	R	T	Y	U	I	O

dance, rain, wings, quacks, bows

What color is Daisy?

What does Daisy love to do?

Who joins Daisy?

Is the weather sunny or rainy?

How does Daisy feel?

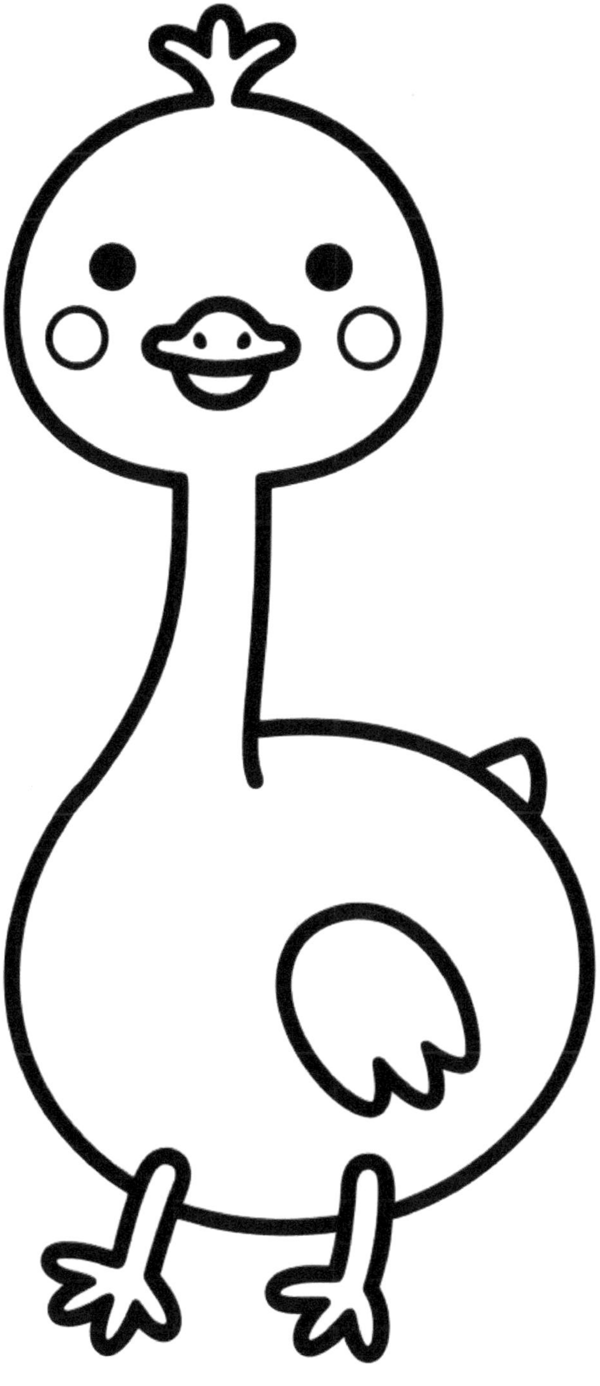

Benny the Busy Bee

Benny is a little bee.
He flies from flower to flower.
He gathers sweet nectar.
The sun shines on his wings.
He sees a butterfly.
They fly together.
Benny finds a
big sunflower.
He buzzes happily.
Then he returns to his hive.
He had a good day.

English Word	**German**
bee	Biene
gathers	sammelt
nectar	Nektar
wings	Flügel
butterfly	Schmetterling
sunflower	Sonnenblume
buzzes	summt
hive	Bienenstock
returns	kehrt zurück
happily	fröhlich

B	E	E	Q	W	E	R	T	Y
N	E	C	T	A	R	S	D	F
L	K	J	H	G	F	D	Z	Z
F	L	O	W	E	R	X	C	V
B	U	Z	Z	E	S	M	N	B
A	S	D	F	G	H	J	K	L
H	I	V	E	Q	W	E	R	T
U	I	O	P	L	K	J	H	G
M	N	B	V	C	X	Z	A	S
Q	W	E	R	T	Y	U	I	O

bee, nectar, buzzes, hive, flower

What kind of insect is Benny?

What does he collect?

Who does he see?

Where does he go at the end?

How does Benny feel?

The Verb 'to be'

- **am ➜** used only with I (I am)
- **is ➜** used with he, she, it, or one thing (A dog is...)
- **are ➜** used with we, you, they, or more than one thing (Dogs are...)

Fülle die Lücken mit der richtigen Form des Verbs 'to be' aus: **am, is,** oder **are**.

- A giraffe ________ very tall.
- I ________ happy when I see my dog.
- Elephants ________ very big animals.
- A snake ________ a long reptile.
- We ________ going to the zoo today.
- The birds ________ singing in the tree.
- A polar bear ________ white.
- You ________ a good friend to your pet.

Present Simple Tense

Erklärung:
Wir benutzen das Simple Present (die einfache Gegenwart), um über Dinge zu sprechen, die immer wahr sind (Fakten) oder die regelmäßig passieren (Gewohnheiten). Tiere sind dafür ein perfektes Thema!

Die magische 'S'-Regel:
Wenn das Subjekt he, she, it oder eine einzelne Sache ist, fügen wir ein -s an das Ende des Verbs hinzu.

- Dogs bark. (Dogs = they)
- A dog barks. (A dog = it)
- Monkeys eat bananas. (Monkeys = they)
- A monkey eats bananas. (A monkey = it)

Kreise das richtige Verb ein, um den Satz zu vervollständigen.

- A cow (eat / eats) grass.
- Fish (live / lives) in water.
- A bird (sing / sings) a song every morning.
- Spiders (catch / catches) flies.
- My cat (sleep / sleeps) on the sofa all day.
- Lions (hunt / hunts) for food.

Fülle die Lücke mit der richtigen Form des Verbs in der Klammer aus. Denk an die magische 's'-Regel!

- A dolphin _______________ (swim) in the ocean.
- Bees _______________ (make) honey.
- My dog _______________ (run) very fast when we play.
- A bear _______________ (sleep) all winter.
- Kangaroos _______________ (live) in Australia.
- The cat _______________ (watch) the birds from the window.
- Horses _______________ (eat) hay and apples.
- A spider _______________ (have) eight legs. (Be careful! This one is irregular.)

Plurals (One and Many)

Erklärung:
Wenn wir über mehr als eine Sache sprechen, ändern wir das Nomen normalerweise von der Einzahl (Singular) in die Mehrzahl (Plural).

Regelmäßiger Plural: Füge einfach ein -s hinzu.

- one dog ➜ two dogs
- one cat ➜ five cats

Unregelmäßiger Plural: Manche Wörter verändern sich auf eine besondere Art. Man muss sie einfach auswendig lernen!

- one mouse ➜ two mice
- one sheep ➜ ten sheep (no change!)
- one fish ➜ three fish (no change!)
- one goose ➜ many geese

Schreibe die Pluralform des Tieres in die Lücke.

- I see one bird, but he sees three ____________ (bird).
- There is one ____________ (mouse) in the kitchen!
- The farm has many ____________ (sheep).
- My aquarium has one big fish and ten little ____________ (fish).
- A cat likes to chase ____________ (mouse).
- The farmer has three horses and two ____________ (goose).

Lies den Satz und kreise das richtige Wort ein.

- I see one (bee / bees) on the flower.
- The zoo has two brown (bear / bears).
- Many (fly / flies) are in the kitchen.
- A group of (wolf / wolves) is called a pack.
- There are ten (fish / fishes) in the tank.
- Two little (puppy / puppies) are playing in the garden.

Benutze 'A' oder 'An'

Schreibe 'a' oder 'an' vor jedes Tier.

- ____ elephant
- ____ cat
- ____ alligator
- ____ bear
- ____ octopus
- ____ owl
- I see ____ big lion.
- It is ____ old turtle.
- That is ____ angry bear.
- A frog is ____ green animal.
- This is ____ orange fish.
- Look! ____ happy dog.
- An owl is ____ interesting bird.

Einen Satz bilden

Lies die Wörter. Schneide sie aus und ordne sie richtig.
Dann schreibe den Satz auf.

Wörter:

see I cat a

Schreibe den Satz:

____

Wörter:

can The run dog

Schreibe den Satz:

____

Wörter:

the   I   bird   like

Schreibe den Satz:

____

Wörter:

is   The   green   frog

Schreibe den Satz:

____

Wörter:

fish   swim   can   The

Schreibe den Satz:

____

Wörter:

ears have big Elephants

Schreibe den Satz:

____

Wörter:

is The white fish

Schreibe den Satz:

____

Wörter:

neck giraffe The a long has

Schreibe den Satz:

____

Ordne das Tier zu

bug

Frog

chicken

sheep

Hippopotamus

Monkey

Chipmunk

Walrus

Octopus

Wähle das richtige Wort

Kreise das richtige Wort ein, das das Tier beschreibt.

- A giraffe is (short / tall).
- A snail is (fast / slow).
- A lion is (weak / strong).
- A mouse is (big / small).
- A rabbit is (fast / slow).
- A cheetah is very (slow / fast).
- A turtle is very (slow / fast).
- A parrot can be very (quiet / noisy).
- A polar bear lives where it is (hot / cold).
- A porcupine is (spiky / soft).
- A butterfly is very (heavy / light).
- A shark can be (dangerous / safe).

Was bin ich?

Lies die Hinweise und schreibe den Namen des Tieres.
Du kannst die Wörter aus der Box benutzen.

Frog	**Monkey**	**Lion**	**Snake**	
Sheep	**Zebra**	**Pig**	**Duck**	**Owl**

- I have no legs. I am long. I say "hiss".

  I am a __________________________.
- I am the "king of the jungle". I am a big cat and I have a loud roar.

  I am a __________________________.
- I can climb trees. I love to eat bananas.

  I am a __________________________.
- I am green. I can jump very high. I live in ponds.

  I am a __________________________.
- I live on a farm. I am pink. I love to roll in the mud and I say "oink".

  I am a __________________________.
- I look like a horse, but I have black and white stripes. I live in Africa.

  I am a __________________________.
- I have big eyes. I am a bird that hunts at night. I say "hoot, hoot".

  I am an __________________________.
- I have soft white wool. I live on a farm with a shepherd. I say "baa, baa".

  I am a __________________________.

Printed in Poland
by Amazon Fulfillment
Poland Sp. z o.o., Wrocław

54709084R00057